Sasha and Penny's Sweet Swap

by Jim MacCurtain

Illustrated by Nadia Ronquillo

Sasha and Penny's Sweet Swap

Written by Jim MacCurtain
Illustrated by Nadia Ronquillo

ISBN: 979-8-9921634-4-5

For my mother Judy, who showed me strength and encouraged me to read, and my daughter Porter, who showed me joy and encouraged me to write.

Chapter 1

Penny shrieked so loudly that Sasha fell out of her chair, her heart racing with fear. "What is it!?" Sasha screamed, hiding under the wooden table that served as their lemonade stand. "We had our first customer, but he had no money and was ugly!" Penny said.

"Wait, what? Was it a robber?" Sasha asked, dusting herself off and standing up, hoping to catch a glimpse of the bad guy running away. "Nope, it was a bumblebee," Penny replied. "It flew straight past my nose, into the pitcher, and took a drink. Or a swim. I'm not sure. Anyway, I thought I was going to be stung for sure. Instead, he just ruined this lemonade!"

Sasha began laughing uncontrollably, bending over and slapping her knee. "HAHAHAHA. Maybe he was attracted to your red hair. He might have thought you were a flower! Well, maybe it's for the best. We haven't sold a single cup, and it's

80 degrees out. We must be doing something wrong. Let's go for a walk and figure it out."

Penny ran inside her large brick house on 6th Street in Park Slope, a leafy green neighborhood in Brooklyn, New York that is filled with huge trees, busy sidewalks, and some of the best food you can imagine. She let her mother know that they were going to shut down the stand for a little while and asked if she would join them for an inspiration walk.

This was not the first nor the last inspiration walk for the girls; it was their go-to approach for problem-solving and coming up with big ideas. The results were legendary. Like last spring, when they overheard their fathers complaining about how boring work at their architecture firm had become, Sasha and Penny had taken an inspiration walk through the

Brooklyn Botanical Gardens. Surrounded by vibrant flowers, Sasha had declared, "Our dads need more color in their lives—look at their clothes, so BLAH!"

Penny's eyes lit up. "Colorful clothes will make them feel more creative and maybe inspire the people they work with too!" The next day, while their dads played tennis at the courts in nearby Prospect Park, Sasha and Penny transformed their fathers' wardrobes into works of art by covering them in paint and glitter. At first, the men were very upset and scolded the girls for ruining their clothes. But they had a good sense of humor and could see that the girls genuinely thought it would be helpful, so they decided to give it a try. Their colorful, mismatched outfits brightened the office and made everyone feel more creative. The other workers got in on the fun, adding colorful buttons to their shirts and stickers to their shoes.

In second grade, after a long inspiration walk, they'd turned a block party into a neighborhood sensation by pretending to be world-famous fortune tellers. Their playful approach had extended the party by hours and left the entire neighborhood buzzing with excitement. The neighbors didn't even mind that these famous fortune tellers were two 8-year-old girls dressed up in their mothers' scarves and sunglasses.

So, on this fine June afternoon nearing the end of third grade, they decided to go on a walk.

Chapter 2

Emma didn't have the heart to tell Dali that she had dropped another carton of eggs. Quietly, she cleaned it up, her tears mixing with the yolks as she mopped the black and white tile floor. Starting a business was hard, especially for someone who had only been a part-time chef before. Once the kitchen was tidy, she splashed some cold water on her lightly freckled face and fixed the bun she had wrapped her long brown hair in.

Emma left the kitchen and went to see Dali in the main room of their new bakery. Dali looked perfect, as always. Her black curls bounced lightly on her shoulders as she rolled another line of paint on the wall. She turned to Emma and smiled broadly. "What do you think? I found a paint called 'Guava Green,' and I just LOVE it," she exclaimed.

Dali's smile faded as she saw the tears in Emma's emerald-green eyes. She rushed to Emma's side. "What is it?" she asked, enveloping Emma in one of her famous hugs. Emma tried to speak clearly, but the words came out jumbled. "THE EGGS… and flour everywhere… I can't even get started cooking because I keep spilling or breaking everything!"

Dali smiled and rubbed Emma's back. This was not the first time Emma had been too hard on herself. "EMMA, look at me. We are JUST starting this thing—we're going to make a lot of mistakes, but if we stick with it, we will get it right. Just hang in there! Forget the eggs; I'm sure we can get some more. What I need to know is if you have decided on a name?"

Dali's eyes sparkled with enthusiasm as she continued, "Do you want to go with 'Something Less Sweet' or 'Virtuous Crumbs'? The name is important, Emma. It's the first thing people will notice about us. I think the parents in this neighborhood are going to be so excited to have a new bakery focused on fewer sweets and healthier treats! We need to stay focused on our mission and make sure the name makes people want to try our creations."

Emma took a deep breath, feeling a bit more reassured by Dali's confidence. "You're right, Dali. We can do this. Let's make 'Virtuous Crumbs' a place where everyone wants to come."

Dali grinned. "That's the spirit! Now, let's get back to work and make this bakery a success."

Chapter 3

This day, like most spring days in Park Slope, was a delight. Bright sun shone through the elm trees on 6th Street, alighting some leaves and providing thin rays of light down to the sidewalk. Many of the houses in the neighborhood were over one hundred years old, and Sasha and Penny loved looking at the gardens that dressed up the front of the buildings with colorful roses, tulips, and occasionally a small bubbling fountain. The girls loved mysteries and wondered what interesting and magical things had happened in these old homes over the years.

As the self-proclaimed biggest dog fans in Brooklyn, Sasha and Penny were never disappointed when they walked around the neighborhood. They encountered big, fluffy white dogs with happy eyes, sunny golden retrievers, and cute little pugs with curly tails and funny names like Mr. Nugget and Rocco. In between petting pups, Sasha and Penny tried to figure out why their lemonade stand wasn't selling well.

"It can't be the taste," Sasha said. "We're using my grandmother's recipe. It's delicious!" And it couldn't be the design, they had decorated their stand beautifully, covering it with sparkles and the name "Sasha and Penny's Tart & Tasty Lemonade Hut" written in big bold letters.

Suddenly, Sasha understood the problem—they were not alone! In their 20-minute walk, they had seen no fewer than four other lemonade stands! Their product was just not unique enough and they needed to come up with something to help it stand out.

"Do you know what might help?" Sasha said, her blue eyes lighting up. "It might be time for an ice cream!" Penny squealed and looked at her mom to see if it was okay. Elizabeth shook her head and smiled. "Sure, here's $10. Just be sure to get something good."

The girls ran to their favorite spot, Sticky Fingers Ice Cream, just around the corner. Sasha got chocolate with rainbow sprinkles and Penny chose strawberry with chocolate sprinkles. As they ate their ice creams, Sasha and Penny brainstormed ideas to make their lemonade stand more unique.

"What if we gave our stand a theme?" Penny suggested. "Like a tropical paradise or an old fashion soda shop?" "That could work," Sasha said, "but we'd need a lot of decorations, and I'm not sure we have enough money for that."

"How about special promotions?" Sasha offered. "We could do a 'buy one, get one free' deal." "Hmm, those are good ideas," Penny said, "but we'd have to sell a lot more to make up for the free ones if we want to make any money!"

They continued to toss around ideas. "What if we had some entertainment at our stand," Sasha suggested. "Like live music or games for kids." Penny nodded thoughtfully. "I love that, but we'd need to find musicians or set up games and we don't have enough time."

Finally, as they licked the last of their ice creams, Penny had an idea. "What if we added fruit infusions to our lemonade?" Sasha's eyes lit up. "Yes! Your house always has fresh berries and oranges. We could crush strawberries to make 'Strawberry Heaven Lemonade' and twist oranges and tangerines to make 'Sunshine in a Cup.' And maybe we could add some seltzer for bubbles. And I think we should bring our Astrology book and Magic 8-Ball to tell people their horoscopes and fortunes-they always love that."

"That sounds so fun!" Penny said excitedly. "Let's do it!"

With a firm plan in mind, they headed back to Penny's house to get started. On the walk, they passed a new bakery on 8th Avenue with a sign indicating it focused on "healthy sweets." Penny laughed, her eyes lighting up with a mischievous grin. "Healthy sweets? Ha! Those are two words that don't go together!"

Chapter 4

"Dali! Can you turn down the music? My mom is on the phone. She wants to hear more about our plans for opening day!" Emma shouted over the booming sounds of the trumpet and piano coming from Dali's music speaker.

Emma and Dali shared an apartment just around the corner from their bakery. It was on the top floor of a charming brownstone building. Their apartment was small but stylish, with dark wood floors and red brick walls. They each had their own room, decorated to reflect their tastes. Emma's room was always a bit messy, adorned with beautiful paintings she had created herself. Dali's room was spotless and filled with plants. Outside of when she was asleep, she always had jazz music playing, especially Miles Davis and Louis Armstrong.

Life had changed dramatically for them lately. They went from working long hours at a bank to owning their own business. After seven years at the bank, they were tired and ready for something new. Over several months of long conversations, a shared dream emerged; they would combine Emma's talent for cooking with Dali's passion for healthy living and design to make a cool, health-conscious bakery. They chose to open it in Park Slope because they lived there and knew no one else had a business quite like theirs.

On opening day for the bakery, the girls quickly ate some fruit and had coffee before bouncing out of their apartment on 9th Street and scurrying towards the bakery. The day was cloudy and windy, but that did not affect their enthusiasm. They were nervous but so excited!

Chapter 5

Dali and Emma's bakery, "Virtuous Crumbs," was a charming little shop on 8th Avenue with a simple, modern design. Shelves lined with gluten-free and vegan goodies gave it a distinct appeal. Healthy teas and matcha were available for purchase—perfect, they thought, to wash down their freshly-baked treats. The bakery was their dream come true—and they believed that Park Slope, with its health-focused residents, would be the perfect location for Virtuous Crumbs to succeed.

The first day went well, with several of their closest friends stopping by after work, and a couple of local nurses and schoolteachers popping in to enjoy the teas and sugar-free pastries. Their friend Andrew stopped by too, impressed with the beautiful bakery. "This is INCREDIBLE, guys. I am so proud of you. But I have to ask, and please don't be mad at me, are kids going to like this stuff?? I didn't start liking apple cider vinegar until I was 28!" Dali grinned and shook off the question. "Don't worry Andrew, we'll be fine," she said. But after the small crowd left, the bakery did get pretty quiet. Dali and Emma were a bit surprised that no hungry teenagers or families with young children came in but tried to remain positive. They were just happy that they had several happy customers and nothing broke.

Business slowed dramatically after the first day, and bad days turned into bad weeks with fewer and fewer people coming into the bakery. They were happy at the end of each day to donate their unsold goods to a local food pantry, but that did not help them pay their bills and they were starting to get scared. Without more sales they would run out of money and have to close the bakery, for good.

Dali frowned as the clock struck 5pm, the time they closed the shop each day. "We haven't had a customer since lunchtime. What do you think is going on, Emma?"

Emma sighed, "I really don't know. I think our stuff is amazing. Should we be staying open later or offering discounts? Or maybe we need to do a better job promoting the store?" Dali wondered out loud if the problem was bigger than that. "Maybe people here aren't as interested in healthy sweets as we thought?"

Emma shook her head. "Eh, I don't think so. This is Park Slope, after all. It's a very healthy neighborhood." Emma looked at Dali, her eyes sad but hopeful. "We'll figure this out. We have to or we are going to go out of business..."

Dali nodded reassuringly. "Absolutely. I don't give up on anything, and I know you don't either. And who knows, magic can happen, right? Maybe we'll get lucky somehow and things will get better. Let's get a good night's sleep and get up early tomorrow so we can brainstorm more."

On their walk home, they passed a cute little lemonade

stand run by two young girls. Dali and Emma were impressed—these girls had put a clever twist on lemonade by infusing it with fresh fruit. And more than that, they offered free horoscopes for customers! Emma and Dali each grabbed a "Strawberry Heaven" lemonade and let the girls tell them their horoscope. Emma and Dali were both Scorpios, born just a few weeks apart in 1995. Like typical Scorpios, they were creative & mysterious, so they weren't too surprised when the girls told them both that strange things were about to happen to them.

Dali turned to Emma and laughed, "How cute was that?! Maybe we should hire those girls to help us out!"

Chapter 6

Every morning, Penny hustled across the street to meet Sasha and her dad for their daily walk to school. The sun was just beginning to rise, casting a golden glow on the large stone building that was located just up the block on Prospect Park West. Their third-grade classroom was located on the top floor and offered a beautiful view of the park.

Sasha and Penny's teacher, Ms. Kingston, ushered them into the classroom after they stored their backpacks in their heavily decorated lockers. "Fifteen minutes of choice time, girls. Enjoy!" she exclaimed, in her typically high-pitched and bubbly voice. The girls loved Ms. Kingston; she had bright blue eyes and big, white teeth that were always on display due to her constant smile.

The girls were the first to arrive that day, so Sasha plopped on the highly coveted purple beanbag and Penny sat cross-legged on the plush, orange-red carpet that perfectly matched her hair while they leafed through their favorite book, "Sorcery

& Magic for True Believers." The book contained magical stories of various men, women, and children from hundreds of years ago that were able to complete incredible feats of magic. There was Juniper Pike, a girl from Ireland that ran with fairies and slid down a rainbow to find the famous pot of gold. Or Claudia Ortiz, an old woman from Puerto Rico who could speak with dolphins and was often found riding them near the seashore on warm mornings. They giggled with delight at these stories and discussed their dreams of doing something magical.

Hunter Healy and Cara Kelley strutted into the room, their eyes immediately landing on Sasha and Penny. The hairs on Sasha and Penny's arms raised and their stomachs filled with butterflies, as they knew they would be teased again. Hunter's smirk widened as he pointed and laughed, "Oh, here we go again with the magic book!" "Haha these two really believe in this stuff, don't they?! They are such weirdos," said Cara.

Penny's face grew bright red, and she clenched her fists tightly. She could feel her blood boiling as Hunter and Cara continued their taunts. Unable to hold it in any longer, at the precise moment Ms. Kingston entered the classroom, Penny screamed, "Shut up! Why don't you two go talk about the crush you have on each other!" For once Ms. Kingston's smile was gone, replaced with a look of disappointment and anger. "Penny, that is totally inappropriate. Please go into the hallway NOW, and you will be spending some time with the principal after our morning meeting." Sasha tried to help but before she could get three words out, Ms. Kingston said, "Sasha, not another word, or you will be joining her." Hunter stood just out of sight of Ms. Kingston so that he could stick out his tongue and snicker at Penny as she left the classroom.

Penny had a long, uncomfortable talk with the principal, who had no interest in her side of the story, but rather demanded she write Hunter and Cara an apology letter. "The nerve!" Penny thought. She rejoined the class at lunch time and sat at a quiet table with Sasha, but she wasn't very hungry. "I am so sick of them Sasha! Somehow, they get away with being mean to everyone and the moment you stand up for yourself, you get in trouble. It's the worst!" Sasha gave Penny a hug and whispered, "Don't worry, we'll figure out how to deal with them one day Pen. We just need a bit of magic to help us."

Chapter 7

Weekday afternoons in Park Slope are bustling and lively. Thousands of kids from a dozen schools head home or to after-school programs—some play basketball, some go for math tutoring. Others join friends at playgrounds or stop for a snack at one of the many stores and restaurants. Adults whiz by in cars and on bikes. Fire trucks, ambulances, and construction workers fill the streets and sidewalks.

One of the more unique, but lesser-known gems about the neighborhood is the opportunity for daily scavenger hunts. Residents often leave unwanted items on the front steps (also known as "stoops") of their buildings. Clothes, books, board games, mirrors, and antique items are routinely placed out front and snatched up for free by passersby. Sasha's dad, Jim, calls it "the ultimate win-win," as homeowners are able to get rid of things without waste, and people find treasures at no cost.

When Penny's mother picked the girls up from school and heard about Penny's woeful day, she suggested a scavenger hunt was in order. They walked up and down some of Park Slope's most beautiful streets—10th Street between 8th Avenue and Prospect Park West, 3rd Street between 7th and 8th—and many more. A gentle breeze kept them cool, and the girls stayed busy chasing squirrels and scouting stoops for treasures.

As they rounded the corner towards Penny's house, they stumbled upon a colorful house with several interesting items laid out on the stoop, and an old woman with a lavender scarf standing nearby. She smiled warmly and suggested they take whatever they would like. Penny found an old copy of an original Baby-Sitters Club book, and Sasha picked up a tennis racket, keen to learn more about a game many of her relatives in Russia played. As Sasha moved a few things around on the steps, a glint of green caught their eyes. It was a rectangular shaped tablet with strange lettering. Intrigued, they approached and picked it up, turning it over and trying to understand what the words said and what the object was for. The old woman stepped closer to them, struck by their focus and interest. She turned to the girls and said, "You girls must love magic and mystery! Well, you have something special in your hands now. When I was younger, I was a college professor and each summer I traveled the world looking for adventure and mystery. That's a replica of an ancient emerald tablet used by scientists interested in the mysteries of the universe thousands of years ago. I picked it up in a small store in Egypt many years ago, when I went to see the Pyramids of Giza. You can have it, but be careful, if

you make a wish while holding the tablet, it's bound to come true."

The girls exchanged looks of delight. "Wow, thank you! We sure do love magic, and we make wishes all time, especially at 11:11 and when we throw coins into fountains. We'll take it! Thank you!" Sasha exclaimed. As they walked away, the old woman smiled and muttered to herself, "May these girls be masters of wonder and delight, and may their wishes come true.!"

Penny's excitement grew; her heart felt as though it was in her throat. They decided to stop at their favorite local diner to examine their find and talk further.

Chapter 8

Dali almost never ate unhealthy foods. She preferred vegetables over burgers and a nice piece of fish instead of pizza. Eating "clean," as she liked to say, helped keep her energy levels high and her skin glowing. So, Emma's jaw almost hit the table at Star Diner when Dali asked the waiter for a plate of piping hot french fries and a milkshake with whipped cream and a cherry. "Hahaha! FRIES, DALI?! Now I know you are stressed out!" Emma shrieked, while turning to the waiter with a smile. "Make that two please!" The women giggled heartily; they were so frustrated and tired with the bakery that they had to laugh, otherwise they would have cried. Emma took a big gulp of her milkshake while Dali poured ketchup on her fries and started to devour them. "Ugh, being a grown up is rough. Sometimes I wish I was a kid again," said Emma. Dali nodded intensely in agreement while making an enormous SLURP, SLURP sound with her straw as she searched for the remaining bits of milkshake.

In the booth just behind Emma and Dali, Sasha and Penny sat with Penny's mother Elizabeth, sharing a Caesar salad and some chicken tenders. The girls chatted excitedly about their day, unaware of the interesting turn their evening was about to take.

Sasha held the tablet close to her face, examining the intricate patterns and mysterious symbols etched into the green plastic. "It's in Arabic," Elizabeth explained. "Unless you're some kind of genius, it might be tough to read it now."

"Well, I bet it says one day two girls are going to change the world!" said Sasha, excitedly. Penny shook her head and added, "That is, if they can find a way to avoid annoying boys and mean girls. I am so sick of dealing with those bullies and on top of it, the principal and Ms. Kingston don't always listen to us when we do have problems." Penny's mom sighed and leaned in closer. "Being a kid can be rough sometimes girls, I totally get it." Sasha agreed, "Sometimes I wish we could just fast forward and be adults, because we are going to do GREAT things. We could start a business or become Doctors or veterinarians!" Penny added, "Definitely! The possibilities are endless and there will not be any bullies to worry about!" She reached across the table with her right arm and gave Sasha a fist bump and a nod.

Sasha pulled back from the fist bump and reached for her fork. Her mind was wandering, and she accidentally knocked the tablet off the table and onto the floor. Penny gasped, worried it would be broken and jumped out of her seat to pick it up. As she leaned down, she came face to face with a pretty woman with brown hair, green eyes, and freckles. "Let me get that for you," Emma said, suddenly realizing she had seen this girl and the friend standing behind her before.

Dali turned and looked at Sasha and Penny and excitedly said, "You are the girls from that cute lemonade stand! You girls rock, we loved your stand! We actually just started a business of our own. It's a healthy bakery called Virtuous Crumbs, on 8th Avenue between 12th and 13th Streets. You guys should stop by sometime! Anyway, what's this you dropped?"

Penny's heart raced as she found herself face-to-face with Emma. Her usual confidence wavered as she rarely spoke to grown-ups that she didn't know, and she froze, her mind blank despite her desire to speak. Sasha jumped in, "Yes that is us, thank you! We live nearby and love this place. We come every Friday afternoon." She turned to Emma and added, "Thanks for picking up our tablet. We just got it." Emma smiled, standing up as she handed the tablet back to Penny. "No problem! What is this thing? It looks super cool and mysterious!"

Sasha smiled, "Well we aren't EXACTLY sure but it's some kind of ancient thing and it's supposed to be magical. We are going to try to make some wishes on it later and see what happens. The woman we got it from said whatever you wish for comes true if you are holding the tablet." Dali laughed gently and said, "That's fun. We were just talking about how we wish we were kids again! Good luck!" Both groups sat back at their table and made small talk while they finished their meal. Elizabeth, Sasha, and Penny finished first and waved goodbye on their way out.

Chapter 9

That night at Penny's house, the girls made brownies smothered in caramel sauce that they enjoyed while watching one of their favorite movies (and books!), Matilda. It was a sleepover night, and movies and desserts were always on the itinerary. Penny's parents liked it too, because seeing Matilda's mean parents in action made Penny appreciate her own parents more. When the movie finished, Penny's dad told them it was time to brush their teeth and get dressed for bed.

As they got ready, they talked excitedly about the day, having long forgotten about the trouble at school and instead focusing on the fun they had on the scavenger hunt and meeting the cool older girls, Dali and Emma, at the diner. "Do you think they liked the tablet?" Penny asked, and Sasha nodded excitedly. "Well, I mean who wouldn't? You can sort of tell it's magical and everyone likes magical stuff. Except for Hunter and Cara, of course!"

Penny snorted, something she did often when she was feeling happy and laughing hard. She picked up the tablet and said, "I wish we could be like Dali and Emma or even trade places with them! They had cool clothes, ate fun food, and were totally grown up. They didn't even have to have their mom or dad sitting with them and they have their own business! That must be amazing." Sasha agreed, briefly taking the tablet from Penny and hugging it close before she gave it back to Penny, who asked if she could sleep with it that night. As they drifted off to sleep, they had no idea how dramatically their lives were about to change.

Chapter 10

Penny woke up after a deep sleep, yawning loudly and rubbing her eyes. The sound of her yawn surprised her—it felt unusually powerful. Stretching her arms over her head, she felt like a giant as her hands bumped into the headboard behind her. But her surprise quickly turned into pure shock. She sat up in an unfamiliar bed, in an unfamiliar room. Reaching up to her hair, she felt soft, bouncy curls and rubbed them slowly against her face, wondering what was going on.

She hurriedly stood up and faced a mirror, and in her shock, mustered up just a whisper full of confusion, "Wait what???" She couldn't believe her eyes—she looked nothing like herself. Instead, she resembled one of the women from the diner—Dali. Tall, with long arms and legs, darker skin, and hot pink nail polish. She briefly smiled at how great she looked but was more concerned with figuring out what was going on because this was CRAZY.

"Where am I?" she thought nervously. "AND WHERE IS SASHA?" she yelled out loud. The door to the room flew open, and an array of colorful hats fell to the ground as it hit the brick wall. A tall brunette with brown hair, freckles, and green eyes stood there, looking just as shocked.

"I AM RIGHT HERE. BUT I AM NOT ME!" the brunette exclaimed. Penny stared in astonishment. "You're not Sasha, you're the woman from the diner, Emma! Where is my friend!?" she shouted, feeling a mix of anger and fear.

The brunette took a deep breath. “Well, Penny, you don’t exactly look like yourself either, you look like Dali! But I’ll prove to you that I’m Sasha. We’ve been best friends since we met in Forest School in Prospect Park. We’re both only children and consider each other sisters, except we rarely fight. You hate snakes, love dogs, and sometimes you laugh so hard that you pee your pants.”

Tears welled up in Penny’s eyes. She ran to her friend and hugged her closely. “What the heck is going on here, Sasha? This is REALLY strange, and I am scared,” she said, her voice wavering.

“I don’t know, Penny, but I bet it has to do with that tablet and our wish to become grownups. The old woman did tell us to be careful with it,” Sasha replied, trying to stay calm.

Chapter 11

Dali woke up startled, her heart pounding. She glanced around, taking in the unfamiliar surroundings. She found herself in a room that was small and cluttered with toys and posters of Taylor Swift. On the wall to her left there was a calendar with images of pug dogs all over it. She was briefly distracted by the image of the pug dressed like a firefighter. She pictured a crew of little pug firefighters trying to hold a big hose and put out a fire and began to giggle. But the funny moment passed, and she sat up quickly, feeling an unusual lightness in her limbs. As she swung her legs over the side of the bed, she noticed they were much shorter than she remembered and that her famous hot pink toenail polish was missing.

"What on earth..." she muttered, her voice sounding oddly high-pitched. She jumped up and ran to the mirror, nearly tripping over an American Girl doll on the floor. The reflection that stared back at her was that of a young girl with long red hair and green eyes.

"This can't be real," she whispered, touching her face and hair in disbelief. "I must be dreaming."

Just then, a body sat up slowly on the top bunk of the bed behind her, and a girl with big, blue eyes, fair skin, and a cascade of thick blonde hair looked down at her. "Emma?" Dali asked cautiously.

"Yes, it's me," Emma replied, her voice shaky and soft. "Dali, what is going on? We're... children? And apparently, I am a blond one, and you are a redhead?" She wasn't sure if she was hallucinating and wanted to laugh at the absurdity of the situation but knew that now was not the time for giggling.

Dali took a deep breath, trying to stay calm. "Okay, let's think this through logically. We were at the diner last night, and we both wished we could be kids again. Do you remember that?"

Emma nodded, looking around the room. "Yes, but I didn't think it would happen! I was kidding! How is this possible?"

Dali frowned, her mind racing. "I don't know, but we need to figure out how to reverse this. Let's look around and see if we can find any clues. There must be an explanation."

They began to search the room, opening drawers and looking under the bed. Dali found a journal with the name "Penny" written on the cover. She flipped through the pages, reading about school projects, friends, and her favorite teacher.

"Oh my God! This must be Penny's room," Dali said, holding up the journal. "It looks like we've swapped places with those girls from the diner. Am I now Penny? I like this red hair. Did you know that only 5% of the world has red hair?"

Emma nodded, picking up a photo of two smiling girls. "Yes, it's really unique, but how can you remember something like that during such a crazy moment? I am apparently SASHA.

Pretty cool name and it sounds mysterious. Like a spy. You think that kid is a spy? AM I NOW A SPY? I have always wanted to be one, I think. Maybe we can create a spy school or something so we can train?”

Dali stood as tall as her new 4 feet, 7 inches body allowed and raised her hand to get Emma under control. “EMMA, WHAT ARE YOU TALKING ABOUT?! STOP IT, this is serious! We need to stay focused. Let’s check the rest of the house. We’ll figure this out.”

As they left the room, they couldn’t help but notice how everything seemed bigger and more intimidating. But with their adult minds and determination, they knew they would find a way to set things right...at least, they hoped they would.

Chapter 12

Penny and Sasha sat on the living room couch in their 'new' apartment. The soft brown leather of the couch was inviting, and the elegant coffee table in front of it looked perfect for placing a drink or snack. Large windows let in the morning sunlight, giving the room a warm, cozy feel. Everything felt very grown-up and sophisticated.

Penny's stomach grumbled. She went to the kitchen to get them some food. "Sasha, they don't have any cereal, waffles, or bread to toast in here! I only see vegetables, beans, and fruits in the refrigerator!" Penny shouted; her frustration evident.

Sasha sighed, missing their usual Saturday morning pancakes with fruit. "OK, well, I guess I'll just have the fruit, hold the pancakes and syrup," she responded dryly.

As they ate some berries and bananas, they discussed a plan. Penny began, her voice tinged with a mix of excitement and nervousness. "Well, first off, this is KIND OF cool. We get to be adults for a while, and I am sure we will figure out a way to switch back. In the meantime, we might as well have some fun with it." Inside, she felt a flutter of anxiety but also a thrill at the possibilities this unexpected twist presented.

"I agree," said Sasha. "Well, we know they own a bakery. I know exactly where it is, it's on 8th Avenue between 12th and 13th Streets, and it's called Virtuous Crumbs. We walked by it the other day. Tough name to be honest. Anyway, maybe we should go there and see if we can find any clues to help us fix this situation. And maybe we can help the bakery while we are there!" She picked up a set of keys from the dining table labeled "VC" and knew they were for the bakery.

Penny nodded. "Sounds good, but I don't know how anyone can run a bakery with no real sweets!" They found some unused toothbrushes wrapped in plastic, opened them up and brushed their teeth. They then rifled through the grown ups' closets and chose the coolest outfits they could find. Penny went with a black and white checkered skirt and a white tank top and paired it with a pink handbag. Sasha found a long blue dress and silver shoes. "We look so grown up!" Sasha said with a smile, and Penny agreed. They dashed out the door and made their way to the bakery.

Just a few blocks away, Emma and Dali heard an adult calling them down for breakfast. Emma's heart raced, nervous that the adults would think she and Dali did something wrong.

Even with a different, smaller body, Dali still recognized the look in Emma's eyes. She may have looked like Sasha, but it was still Emma in there, her eyes alight with energy and nerves.

Dali spoke to her calmly and said, "Take a breath. For now, you are Sasha, and I am Penny, and we don't need to freak anyone out until we get to the bottom of this. Let's just go downstairs and act like a couple of kids."

Emma nodded. "Ok, PENNY, that sounds good. Although I don't really know how to act like a 9-year-old, it's been a while."

Even when she was wrong, Dali's confidence never wavered. She said, "Ok SASHA, we'll just act incredibly silly and cause a bit of trouble. That's what 9-year-olds do, right? We'll be fine!" Taking a deep breath to steady their nerves, they quickly ran down the long stairs and into the kitchen, their footsteps echoing on the dark wooden floors in the unfamiliar house.

As they reached the bottom, the smell of a sweet breakfast greeted them, causing them to pause before entering the room. Emma turned to Dali and whispered, "I don't think we'll be having any chia seed pudding or matcha today." Dali laughed, gathered herself, and walked into the kitchen, almost shouting, "GOOD MORNING!"

Chapter 13

Penny felt so grown-up walking around Park Slope with a fancy handbag. She had a lot of experience putting on makeup from hours of playing dress-up with Sasha, so she decided to apply some of Dali's purple lipstick and eye shadow. When she saw her reflection in the glass window of a store they passed on the way to the bakery, she got so excited that she practically floated the rest of the way.

Arriving at "Virtuous Crumbs," Sasha reached into Emma's wicker bag and fumbled with the keys as she tried to unlock the door. She hadn't used keys too often in her life, so it took several tries, but eventually, the door unlocked. The two girls, looking very much like women, walked into the bakery and turned on the lights, taking in the sophisticated atmosphere.

Just down the road, chaos ensued at Penny's house. Dali did her best impression of a 9-year-old, breezing past her "mother," opening the refrigerator, and grabbing a canister of whipped cream. Shaking it violently, she loudly sang "Wonderland" by Taylor Swift and squirted whipped cream into her mouth. Penny's mother stood in shocked silence, her jaw open and her eyes bulging.

Dali then walked across the room and sprayed the remainder of the can right in Emma's face, laughing maniacally. At first, Emma froze, unsure of how to handle the situation. But she figured Dali must know more about how to act like a 9-year-old than she did, so she decided to play along. She reached into a bowl of blueberries in the middle of the kitchen table and flung them across the room with her left hand, grabbing a pancake with her right hand and throwing it into the nearby living room like a frisbee.

“MONKEY SEE, MONKEY DO!” Emma yelled, joining in the chaos.

“GIRLS, WHAT ON EARTH ARE YOU DOING?! You are 9 years old, NOT 4! This behavior is completely unacceptable!” Penny’s mother shrieked, her face getting redder with each word.

Chapter 14

Back at Virtuous Crumbs, Sasha and Penny were looking through the large refrigerator filled with items made the day before.

"I guess we can just put these things out for display?" Penny said, looking bewildered at her options. "Cauliflower muffins? Broccoli bread? Brownies made of dates? Yuck! No sugar or flour or chocolate in a brownie—I can't believe this," she sighed. Despite how much they did not like these "healthy desserts," they had no other options than to put them out and hope for the best.

Sasha wiped down the counters with a wet rag and swept a bit of dust from under the stools. "The stools look like they have never been moved," she shouted across the room to Penny. They were unsure how to use the cash register, but with no customers for hours, that was hardly their problem.

On the counter, Sasha found a notebook that showed how much money the bakery was making, and next to it in red ink was a list of all of the bills that they had to pay: rent, electricity, and supplies and equipment they bought. The amount of money they owed was a lot more than the amount of money they were making, which explained a note written under the numbers that said, "We will be out of business soon."

Penny sat down next to Sasha. "Wow, this bakery is really struggling, I feel bad for Dali and Emma. Opening this store must have been a lot of work and a big dream for them, but it's not very successful. We need to do something to help them, but I am not sure where to start."

Sasha nodded in agreement. "Yes. There is so much to do. It doesn't feel that fun in here, so we need to fix that. But we must start with the food. I know they don't want a bakery that has only junk food, but there must be something better than cookies made from chia seeds."

Penny took a deep breath and suggested they go for an inspiration walk in Prospect Park. Along the way, Penny was quiet as she pictured some of the great bakeries she had been to in New York, incredible things her grandmother made, and some places she had seen on a family trip to Paris the year before. She also spent time thinking about Dali and Emma's goal of making healthy treats and wondered how she could help with that but do it in a better way that customers would really enjoy. They stopped and sat on a bench at the edge of the park to talk. "I think I have a starting point for us," she said excitedly. "What's sweet and delicious, but good for you?" she asked Sasha, who looked at her with a puzzled glance. "I mean, I usually don't think of sweet and good for you in the same sentence..." her voice trailed off as she thought. Her mind raced, searching for the answer, and she began to think of her favorite fruit.

"Oh, I see, you are thinking of MANGO! Love it. We'll make it a Mango Bakery. Great idea, Pen!" Sasha exclaimed.

Penny laughed heartily, bending over and clutching her stomach. "No, Sasha, I am not thinking of a Mango Bakery! Ha! But you are on the right track. I am thinking we start making some desserts that have a bunch of brightly colored, fresh fruit, like a fruit tart. We'll still have the delicious crust, but maybe we use less sugar and let the fruit provide the sweetness. What do you think?"

Sasha smiled and gave Penny a fist pump. "Love it, let's do this!" They jumped up from the park benches and headed back to the bakery.

Sasha grabbed the iPad that was placed behind the counter and went to the website her mother often used for cooking and baking recipes. Sasha's mother was an amazing cook, and she had taught Sasha a lot over the last few years. Every Sunday afternoon, they spent time together making dinner and a delicious dessert, with Sasha's mother teaching her about how to measure and mix ingredients and carefully use the oven. She found a recipe for a fruit tart and checked to see if they had all the ingredients. On a positive note, Dali and Emma had stocked the refrigerator with fresh strawberries, bananas, and kiwi, and there was a bag of coconut flour they could use to substitute for regular flour. However, she couldn't find any butter or sugar. She continued her search and found some olive oil, which she thought might be used instead of butter, and a very small bottle of molasses that she figured could replace the sugar.

Sasha and Penny worked together to try to make the fruit tart: cutting the fruit, following the step-by-step directions, mixing everything together, and very carefully putting it in a pie pan inside the oven, which was set to 400 degrees. Sasha was a bit nervous to use the oven, but she had been taught very well and took good care. While it baked, they found some money in a drawer and went next door to the convenience store to buy some eggs, flour, unsalted butter, and brown sugar, knowing that they would need it immediately. They also picked up some lollipops and sat outside the bakery, talking and enjoying their treat.

Almost an hour had passed before it occurred to them to check on the fruit tart. They walked inside the bakery and into the kitchen. Penny placed their groceries on the stainless-steel island while Sasha shut off the stove and opened the door with the big oven mitts that Dali and Emma had hung nearby. She shrieked as she discovered a fruit tart that wasn't bright and colorful at all. It was completely burnt and blackened!

"Oh no!!" she shouted, turning to Penny. "Ugh, I overcooked it. I forgot to set a timer. Now I know why my mother says I can only use the oven when she's around! This is going to be harder than I thought."

Penny couldn't help but laugh. "Well, at least we didn't burn the bakery down—that's a start!"

Sasha chuckled and then sighed, realizing in that moment how difficult their challenge was. "Well, I shut the stove off. Let's take a break and then give it another try," she said, nervous but hopeful.

Chapter 15

Dali's now very little hands were shaking as Penny's mother continued to yell at them about their behavior. She hated getting into trouble. As a child, Dali rarely got into mischief, but when she did, her parents were very strict. Once, during a vacation to visit family in the Dominican Republic, she and another girl decided to use their paint kit to paint designs all over the walls of the hotel room they were staying in. Her mother had been furious, yelling loudly and punishing her with no TV for a month. The memory of that day flashed through her mind, intensifying her anxiety. She wanted to apologize quickly and profusely, but in her panic, she almost revealed that she was not, in fact, Penny.

"Mom, I am so sorry. I don't know what has gotten into me. I just felt like this is what kids do!" Dali stammered, her voice shaking.

Emma, with eyes bulging in shock, stepped in to rescue her friend. "Oh, Penny, stop playing around. Sorry, Mrs. M. We were just being silly last night. We played family, and I acted like a young girl, and Penny here, well, she pretended to be a grown-up. Then we switched places and just got a bit confused. We'll clean everything up, and it won't happen again."

Dali nodded in agreement and quietly whispered, "Thanks, Emm...I mean Sasha."

Penny's mother considered a punishment but saw the regret in the girls' eyes. Deciding to let them clean up and move on from the incident, she sighed. "Just clean up this mess. I don't want to see anything like this again."

The girls set to work cleaning up the kitchen, the atmosphere tense but gradually easing as they worked together. As they wiped whipped cream off the walls and picked up scattered blueberries, Dali couldn't help but feel a bit of relief. Emma's quick thinking had saved them.

While cleaning, they whispered about their plan for Monday. "We need to lay low tomorrow," Emma said, glancing over her shoulder to make sure Penny's mother wasn't listening. "We'll get ready for school and keep our heads down. On Monday morning, we'll meet for the walk to school together and talk more."

Dali nodded. "Yes, and at some point, we need to track

down the real Sasha and Penny. Hopefully they will be at the bakery or our apartment. I hope they are OK; they must be in shock!"

Emma hugged Dali close. "We'll sort it out. It's just going to be a little weird and will take a few days, that's all. But we've got this."

Chapter 16

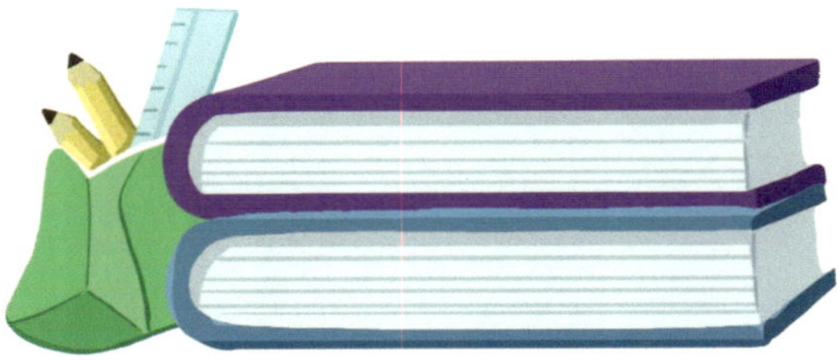

Dali yawned and stretched her pint-sized arms and legs. Despite how crazy swapping places with Penny was, after a couple of days, she did find herself beginning to enjoy it. Her small bed was cozy, and she hugged Penny's "stuffies" close. She remembered lying in bed as a child many years ago, petting her stuffed Dalmatian, "Lovey," and whispering secrets in its ear. Sometimes she would tell it about new ideas she had for magic potions, other times she would tell it about things that made her afraid. No one had ever listened to her as carefully as Lovey did, so the little pup would always hold a special place in her heart. She smiled and looked around the room at the pink curtains and that pug calendar. "Pug Firefighters! HA!" she thought. It was already 7:30 and she could hear "mother" yelling up to her to get dressed quickly. She hurriedly put on some shorts and a fun, lavender t-shirt and brushed her hair into a ponytail.

After a quick bowl of oatmeal and fruit, Dali ran across the street to Sasha's house, whose mother was standing in the doorway unknowingly waving to a 29-year-old trapped inside a 9-year-old's body. Sasha's father walked the girls to school and along the way made jokes just like their fathers used to make. Some were funny, and some were so bad, but they enjoyed listening to them either way. It was a welcome distraction from the butterflies they both had in their stomachs. It had been over 20 years since these grown women had been in the 3rd grade, and their memories of the time had been reduced to visions of moments and floods of feelings.

Dali had grown up nearby in Flushing, Queens, another part of New York City, and Emma grew up just outside Boston in a town called Milton. They both generally remembered 3rd grade fondly, filled with friends, fun projects, and sweet teachers. But like almost every other kid ever, they had to deal with their share of challenges, which typically came in the form of other kids. For Dali, it was a boy named Rafa, who used to pull her hair and throw marshmallows at her during lunch time when the teachers weren't looking. She later learned he liked her and just wanted some attention, but at the time he was the bane of her existence. For Emma, it was girls in the 4th grade that teased her often, calling her freckle face and saying she was terrible at soccer. At the time, these insults hurt and made her feel lonely. Looking back, she understood that the insults came from jealousy. Not only was Emma not bad at soccer, but she was amazing; even in the 3rd grade she was better than all the 4th and 5th grade girls and most of the boys! She went on to play soccer

Sasha and Penny's Sweet Swap

Written by Jim MacCurtain
Illustrated by Nadia Ronquillo

ISBN: 979-8-9921634-3-8

Chapter 19

Sasha and Penny hurried into Emma and Dali's apartment, each rushing to their bathrooms to clean up after their long day. Sasha found coconut flour caked in her hair and dusted over her hands, while Penny scrubbed away the stubborn streaks of marker and flecks of glitter clinging to her arms. After a quick change into fresh clothes—a pair of comfy pants and soft sweatshirts—they met in the living room.

Sasha collapsed onto the couch, but then sprung up almost immediately, her energy too restless to allow her to sit still. She paced back and forth, her voice tinged with both hope and anxiety. "Do you think this will actually work, Penny? Will everything go back to normal?"

Penny pulled gently at Sasha's oversized sweatshirt and attempted to redirect her friend's spiraling thoughts. "Sasha, slow down. Yes, you will get to see your parents again, and yes, we'll have pancakes at my house. We just need to follow the plan: sit in the same booth, order fries and milkshakes, and recreate everything from last week."

Taking a deep, steadying breath, Sasha nodded. "Got it, let's do this." They grabbed their essentials and dashed out the door, headed for the diner.

Across town, Emma and Dali ran into some trouble as Penny's mom refused to take them to the diner. Her arms were crossed as she shook her head firmly. "Absolutely not, girls. I'm exhausted. Plus, you just came from a bakery. How could you possibly be hungry?"

Emma felt a rare flutter of helplessness ripple through her; it had been a long time since she had to ask a parent to take her to a restaurant, or anywhere for that matter. She exchanged a desperate glance with Dali, whispering, "What do we do? We MUST get to the diner—and quickly!"

Dali turned on her most endearing, wide-eyed plea. "Mom, we understand you're tired, so how about a deal? If you take us, we'll come straight home and clean up the entire living room—vacuuming and everything. Plus, we'll wash the dishes."

Elizabeth raised an eyebrow, skepticism written all over her face. "Really? You two? Cleaning?" Determined, Dali pressed on. "Yes, we promise. It's only fair if you help us out that we return the favor." After a moment's hesitation,

Elizabeth relented, a small smile breaking through. "Alright, two minutes, and we're out the door." Dali ran upstairs and grabbed the green tablet, which had been carefully placed under her pillow for days.

At the diner, Sasha, Penny, Emma and Dali, now looking very differently than they did a week ago, sat in the same booths as the week before and ordered the same items. Penny loved the sound of the crunch of her hot fries and the sweet, creamy taste of the milkshake. Dali, sitting across from Penny's mom, ate a big Caesar salad, happy to be eating something bright and green.

Emma gently kicked her and stared down at the tablet, encouraging her to get going. Dali nudged the tablet off the edge of the table and watched as it fell to the floor, halfway between their booth and the one next to them. As Dali leaned down to pick it up, she was met by Penny, who kneeled to help. Emma and Sasha stood behind them, nervously smiling. "Ah the girls from the lemonade stand, nice to see you!" Penny said, barely holding in her laugh as she passed the tablet to Dali. "And you still have that magical tablet that makes wishes come true. How wonderful! My friend and I were just talking about a wish that we REALLY hope comes true." Emma chimed in, "Well we sure have a lot in common because we ALSO have a wish that we really hope comes true!"

The four of them giggled and gave each other fist bumps and crossed their fingers at the exact same time. Emma whispered to Penny, "If this works, and I think it will, just try

to come by the bakery tomorrow." Penny smiled and agreed, and they all left the diner.

On the way out, they failed to notice the tiny old woman sitting in the booth behind them, who smiled as she watched the scene unfold and whispered, "May their wishes come true."

Chapter 20

Penny awoke frozen with fear. She dared not open her eyes, afraid that she might find herself in Dali's room, stuck forever as a grown up. She had enjoyed the challenge of being a grown up for a few days, and helping save Virtuous Crumbs, but she wanted to be a kid again. The urge to stretch was strong, but she resisted, worried her hands might find the unfamiliar wooden headboard of Dali's bed instead of the soft edges of her own. Deep down, a small voice urged her to look for the silver lining—to imagine what could go right instead of wrong. Gathering her courage, Penny slowly opened one eye, then the other, and exhaled a sigh of overwhelming relief as waves of red hair hung over her shoulders and the familiar sights of her room came into focus—the Taylor Swift calendar, her cherished collection of stuffed animals, and the pug calendar. Joy bubbled up inside her as she saw Sasha, still sleeping soundly nearby. She couldn't contain herself; she leaped from her bed, dashed over to Sasha, and shook her awake. "Wake up! Wake up! It worked! We're back, Sasha!" Sasha sat up and shook her head, slightly confused after such a deep sleep, but quickly recognized that their wish had come true, and they had gotten their lives back. She began dancing wildly, hugging Penny and shouting "WOOHOO" at the top of her lungs. After the burst of excitement, the girls got dressed and ready for breakfast, where they spread thick cream cheese on toasted bagels and talked about their plan for going down to the bakery to see Dali and Emma that afternoon.

Meanwhile, Emma lay still in her own bed, her eyes closed against the morning light. The last week had been a welcome break from the stress of being a grown up, but she had been 9 before, and that part of her life was behind her. She was ready to get back to pursuing her dreams as a grown woman. Slowly the soft rhythms of John Coltrane's album, "A Love Supreme," filled the air. With that music playing, she knew there was only one place she could be, home! Tears of joy and relief ran down her cheeks. She finally dared to look at her reflection in the mirror across the room—her long brown hair falling gently on her shoulders and green eyes sparkling. She quickly dried her eyes, ran a brush through her hair, and headed to the living room to find Dali.

Their reunion was quiet but filled with deep understanding and relief. They shared a long look, each recognizing the extraordinary journey they had undergone. "Well, that was easily the craziest thing that ever happened to me, and to think I actually wished for it to happen," Emma confessed as she hugged Dali. "Let's never take our normal lives for granted again."

Dali laughed softly, nodding in agreement. "Yes! And now, let's go check on our bakery. Those girls have turned it upside down—in the best way possible."

Chapter 21

Emma and Dali burst through the front door of their bakery with energy and determination. They were inspired by the work that young Sasha and Penny had done to improve their bakery and save it from going out of business. It made sense, after all, that kids might be more interested in coconut bites drizzled in dark chocolate and served with a side of strawberries than they would be in tofu & almond cookies. And that the decorations needed to be colorful and give kids a sense that this was a fun place to be. Now, with more sales and more interested customers, they had a chance to truly make their dreams come true. They sat down to finish their coffees and discussed additional recipes that would fit the new model, like an oatmeal & cherry crumble pie, and some additional activities for families to enjoy, including a prize wheel that kids could spin to win a free treat.

Meanwhile, Sasha and Penny set out for the bakery at 3pm, with Sasha's dad, Jim, trailing behind. He was tall and handsome, with an easy smile and a love of books. Sasha knew that one of his secrets was that he hoped one day to write one himself. If he only knew what had happened over the last week, then he would really have something to write about!

As they turned a corner, Sasha and Penny suddenly came face to face with their enemies, Hunter and Cara. They prepared themselves for insults but were surprised to see bright smiles. "Hi girls!" said Cara. "Yesterday was so funny, I hope we can do something like that again." Hunter nodded in agreement, "Ya, that was a pretty good trick you guys pulled off, I didn't know you had it in you. I was thinking maybe next time we play 'capture the flag' in gym class, we can super glue our flag to the ground so the other team can't steal it!" "HA, that's a good one! Well, we have to go girls, talk soon!" said Cara, as she gave Penny a high five. Penny and Sasha stood motionless, in disbelief at what had just taken place. "Wow, Emma and Dali worked some kind of magic with those two!" Penny said, excitedly. Sasha agreed, "We owe them for sure. It seems like we can start fresh with Hunter and Cara and just focus on having fun together, and maybe causing just a little bit of trouble!" They both laughed and continued to the store.

A tiny, older woman stepped into the bakery wearing a broad purple hat and dark sunglasses. She looked around the bakery and smiled, impressed with all that she saw. She quietly ordered tea and a slice of banana bread and sat at a table near the entrance.

Sasha and Penny entered shortly after the woman and were greeted with hugs and hellos from Dali and Emma. Jim was a bit surprised that these women knew his daughter and her BFF, but only just so. Wherever Sasha and Penny went, they made a big impression. The four girls caught up, sharing the relief about switching back, appreciation for what each of them had done for each other, and excitement about what would come next. Emma and Dali had a few more ideas about how the girls could get along with Hunter and Cara, and Sasha couldn't help but suggest that they add some iPads with kid-friendly games to play. After their chat, Jim motioned to Sasha and Penny that it was time to go. For all of his good qualities, he was a bit impatient and seemed ready to leave.

The old woman, who had been listening in the whole time, stood up and addressed them while Dali, Emma, Sasha, and Penny looked on, confused. "Well, you all have had quite a week, what with the green tablet and swapping places and all. I told you that it made wishes come true!" A bead of sweat dripped down Dali's forehead, as Emma grabbed her hand tightly. Sasha and Penny looked on, jaws and eyes wide open in disbelief, recognizing the woman as the one they got the tablet from during their scavenger hunt last week. The woman walked to the front door, ready to leave. Before she walked out, she turned back one last time and wished them all good luck.

Sasha and Penny looked at each other and then at Dali

and Emma. It was clear that they had something to say but were hesitant. "What is it, girls? Don't be shy, we all know each other way too well at this point," said Emma. Sasha turned and quietly offered, "Umm, well. You know there is just one more thing that needs to change here but we don't want to hurt your feelings," to which Penny added, "And the truth is while we know what the problem is, we don't know the solution." Dali, perplexed and eager to hear, hurriedly said, "Come on girls what is it? What's the problem?" At the exact same moment Sasha and Penny exclaimed "The name!", with Penny adding, "Sorry, but Virtuous Crumbs is just not good. It's too long and it's not fun." Emma and Dali, a bit dejected, turned to each other with sad but accepting eyes. "I think we know what you mean. With all these great changes, Virtuous Crumbs just doesn't apply any more, but what can we call it?" They all offered up ideas, from "Berry Delicious" to "Tart and Tasty," but nothing moved them.

Suddenly, a brightness came over Penny's face and she whispered in Sasha's ear, who nodded with excitement. "We've got it!" said Sasha, with Penny shouting "SWEET SWAP!"